HEALTHY FOOD
CHOICES

Breakfast

Vic Parker

Chicago, Illinois

To contact Capstone Global Library, please call
800-747-4992, or visit our web site
www.capstonepub.com

Edited by Rebecca Rissman, Dan Nunn, and
    Diyan Leake
Designed by Philippa Jenkins
Original illustrations © Capstone Global
    Library Ltd 2014
Picture research by Tracy Cummins
Production by Helen McCreath
Originated by Capstone Global Library Ltd
Printed and bound in China

17 16 15 14 13
10 9 8 7 6 5 4 3 2 1

Library of Congress Cataloging-in-Publication Data
Parker, Victoria, author.
  Breakfast / Vic Parker.
      pages cm.—(Healthy food choices)
  Summary: "Read Breakfast to learn how to make
healthy food choices during this important meal.
Different photos show healthy and unhealthy breakfast
options, while simple text explains why some choices
are better than others. A breakfast foods quiz
concludes the book."—Provided by publisher.
  Includes bibliographical references and index.
  ISBN 978-1-4329-9116-6 (hb)—ISBN 978-1-4329-
9121-0 (pb) 1. Nutrition—Juvenile literature. 2.
Breakfasts—Juvenile literature. 3. Health—Juvenile
literature. I. Title.
  TX355.P254 2014
  613.2—dc23   2013015688

J
PARKER

Acknowledgments
We would like to thank the following for permission
to reproduce photographs: Capstone Publishers
(Karon Dubke) pp. 6, 7, 8, 9, 10, 11, 12, 13, 14,
15, 16, 17, 18, 19, 20, 21, 22, 23, 24, 25, 26, 27;
ChooseMyPlate.gov p. 29 (with thanks to USDA's Center
for Nutrition Policy and Promotion); Getty Images p. 4
(Shannon Fagan), Shutterstock p. 5 (© bikeriderlondon).

Cover photograph of a bowl of children's cereal
and milk reproduced with permission of Shutterstock
(© Hong Vo) and whole grain cereal with fruit
reproduced with permission of Getty Images
(Donald Erickson).

Contents

Some words are shown in bold, **like this.** You can find out what they mean by looking in the glossary.

Why Make Healthy Choices?

Your body runs on food and water. You need food to think, move, and grow. Healthy foods give your body lots of **nutrients**. However, if you eat unhealthy foods, you will not feel or look your best.

Eating healthy foods can help your body fight disease.

Don't forget to brush after meals to keep your teeth healthy!

toothbrush

Your body needs different kinds of foods, in the right amounts for your age and size, to work properly. If you eat healthy foods, you will have lots of energy. You will be able to think quickly and clearly. You will look good, too.

What Makes a Breakfast Healthy or Unhealthy?

It is important to eat breakfast to wake your body up after sleeping and get it going again. Some breakfasts are much less healthy than others. For instance, bagels can be high in **sodium**, which is bad for your heart.

Buttery croissants are high in **saturated fat**, which can damage your heart and blood vessels.

Some foods are low in calories. Others are high in calories.

2 slices of **whole grain** toast with unsweetened fruit spread
300 calories

2 slices of whole grain toast with chocolate hazelnut spread
550 calories

The energy food gives is measured in **calories**. Everyone needs a certain number of calories per day to stay healthy, depending on your age, your size, and how active you are. However, eating too many calories at meals and snack times can make you **overweight**.

7

Processed Cereals

Cereals are a great breakfast choice, since they give us lots of energy. However, many cereals made for children are high in sugar and **calories**. Some healthy-looking breakfast cereals are also high in **sodium**.

Whole milk makes your breakfast high in unhealthy **saturated fat**.

whole milk

added sodium

high in fat

added artificial **colorings**

added sugar

nonfat milk

bran cereal

wheat cereal

Whole grain cereals contain slow-release energy, which keeps us going for longer. They are packed with the **vitamins** and **minerals** your body needs to grow and repair itself. They are a good source of **fiber,** which keeps your **digestive system** working well.

Granola, Muesli, and Oatmeal

Granola and muesli contain healthy **whole grains**, nuts, fruits, and seeds. However, store-bought granola is toasted in oil and sugar, which makes it high in fat and **calories**. Muesli is raw, but store-bought muesli often contains a lot of added sugar and **sodium**.

muesli with added sugar and sodium

Some muesli and granola contain more sugar than sugary breakfast cereals.

granola baked in sugar and hydrogenated vegetable oil

muesli with raw nuts and dried fruit

granola baked in maple syrup and olive oil

oatmeal, honey, nuts, raisins

Make your oatmeal with low-fat or nonfat milk to keep the fat content down.

It is easy to make healthier granola and muesli at home. Always use raw nuts and seeds, and rely on dried fruit for sweetness instead of sugar. Oatmeal is a very healthy choice for a hot whole grain cereal.

Toast

Bread is a good food choice for breakfast, since it contains **carbohydrates** that give us energy. However, some types of bread are much healthier than others. **Whole grain** bread has **fiber, vitamins**, and **minerals** in it. In white bread, many of these healthy things have been taken out.

jam

butter

white toast

White bread with butter and jam is fatty and sugary, without many healthy things for your body.

Whole grain bread is also healthier because it gives us energy that is released slowly. Use low-fat spread on toast instead of high-fat butter. Unsweetened fruit spread is better for you than sugary jam.

For a healthier choice, avoid fatty spreads and just have fruity toppings.

mashed banana

fruit topping

whole grain bread

Eggs

Some foods, such as meat, fish, chicken, and beans, are rich sources of **protein**. Your body needs protein to make skin, muscle, and other tissues. Eggs are high in protein, but they can also be high in fat if they are cooked in an unhealthy way.

Eggs can be good for us, but not if unhealthy ingredients are added.

high-fat butter

added high-fat cheese

white toast

scrambled eggs fried in high-fat butter

hard-boiled egg

Eggs are rich in **antioxidants**. These are natural substances that strengthen the body's ability to fight disease.

low-fat spread

whole grain toast

Eggs cooked in a low-fat way are an excellent breakfast choice. Like other protein foods, eggs take longer to go through the **digestive system** and can keep you feeling fuller for longer. Eggs are also rich in **vitamins** and **minerals**.

Breakfast Sandwiches

Fast-food breakfast sandwiches can look tempting, but they are usually high in **saturated fat**, **sodium**, and **calories**. Also, nearly everything in them is **processed** and they may have unhealthy **artificial additives**.

Processed foods may have **flavoring**, **coloring**, and **preservatives** added to them. These are **chemicals** that have few **nutrients** and can even be harmful.

processed white flour

fatty fried egg

processed cheese

processed sausage meat

You can make a healthier breakfast sandwich at home. Use **whole grain** bread for slow-release energy, **fiber**, **vitamins**, and **minerals**. Top it with low-fat ingredients, such as grilled tomatoes or mushrooms and a **poached** egg or **lean** meat for **protein**.

whole grain English muffin

A homemade breakfast sandwich can be both healthy and delicious.

lean bacon

poached egg

Pancakes and Waffles

Pancakes and waffles are both made from batter containing milk, eggs, and flour. If whole milk and white flour are used, the pancakes and waffles become high in fat (especially if fried in oil) and low in **vitamins** and **minerals.**

white flour, sugary syrup, high-fat whipped cream

white flour, sugary syrup, sugary jam

Unhealthy toppings are often added to pancakes and waffles.

strawberries

blueberries

maple syrup

oatmeal pancakes

low-fat natural yogurt

whole grain-flour waffles

Use just a little maple syrup to add sweetness without too many **calories**.

Pancakes and waffles are healthier if they are made with **whole grain** flour and lower-fat milk. Make them even better for you by adding healthy toppings such as fresh fruit, low-fat natural yogurt, and maple syrup, a natural sweetener containing many **nutrients** that fight disease.

Fruity Breakfasts

Fruit is full of **vitamins** and **minerals**. However, it is not healthy when it is turned into high-sugar jam in layers of high-fat pastries, like toaster pastries.

sugary jam, artificial **coloring**

pastry high in **saturated fat**

Toaster pastries are high in calories, with few **nutrients** for your body.

Rice cakes keep you from feeling hungry.

peanut butter

unsweetened raspberry spread

mashed banana

rice cake

strawberries, blueberries, and low-fat yogurt

Rice cakes will give you the crunch of a toaster pastry, but they are much lower in fat and **calories.** Choose the unflavored type and add your own fruity toppings for lots of vitamins, minerals, and **fiber**—either unsweetened fruit spread or chopped fresh fruit.

Cooked Breakfasts

On a cold day, a big cooked breakfast can warm you and fill you up until lunchtime. It can give you energy, **protein**, **vitamins**, **minerals**, and **antioxidants**. However, if your cooked breakfast is fried, it can be a meal incredibly high in **saturated fat** and **calories**.

Using an animal fat such as butter for frying is an unhealthy cooking method.

fried hash browns

fried fatty bacon

fried eggs

fried pork sausage

whole grain toast with low-fat spread

grilled lean bacon

A cooked breakfast can be healthy.

poached eggs

grilled vegetarian sausage

For a healthier breakfast, cook **lean** meat using low-fat cooking methods such as grilling and poaching. Swap your meat sausage for a vegetarian sausage to add vitamins, minerals, and **fiber**. Swap hash browns for **whole grain** toast to give you energy that is slowly released throughout the morning.

Drinks

Milk contains **calcium** for strong bones and teeth, as well as **protein** for healthy skin and muscles. Fruit juices are packed with **vitamins** and **minerals**. However, some milk is high in fat, and store-bought fruit juices can have lots of added sugar.

Whole milk and store-bought juices can be high in **calories**.

fruit **concentrate**, with added syrup, sugar

whole milk

Swap whole milk for low-fat or nonfat milk to get all the health benefits, with less fat and sugar. Even fresh fruit juice is not as good as eating the whole fruit, so just have it in small amounts. Water is always a great choice of drink. Every part of your body needs water to work properly.

low-fat milk

nonfat milk

Unsweetened drinks are much better for your teeth than sugary drinks.

water

fresh fruit juice

Food Quiz

Take a look at these breakfasts. Can you figure out which picture shows an unhealthy breakfast and which shows a healthy breakfast, and why?

spinach and mushroom omelette fried in a little sunflower oil

water

whole grain toast with low-fat spread

breakfast pizza topped with cheesy scrambled eggs and pieces of fried bacon and sausage

store-bought fruit smoothie

The answer is on the next page.

Food Quiz Answers

This is the healthy breakfast. The vegetable omelette is high in **protein**, **vitamins**, **minerals**, and **antioxidants**. The **whole grain** toast will give you **fiber**, vitamins, minerals, and energy that is slowly released. Water is essential for everything in your body to work properly.

This is the unhealthy breakfast. White-flour pizza dough is high in **sodium** and lacks fiber, vitamins, and minerals. Cheesy scrambled eggs and fried bacon and sausage are high in **saturated fat**. Store-bought smoothies can be packed with sugar, fat, and **artificial additives**. Did you guess correctly?

Tips for Healthy Eating

Use this MyPlate guide to choose the right amounts of different foods for good health. Choose low-fat cooking methods and do not add salt (it is high in **sodium**). Don't forget to drink several glasses of water and to exercise every day.

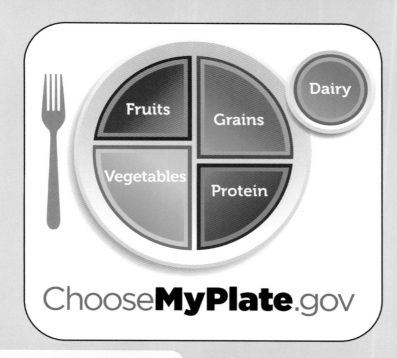

ChooseMyPlate.gov

See if you can get the right balance over the course of a whole day.

Glossary

antioxidant substance that helps your body fight off disease

artificial additive human-made substance that is added to food, such as coloring, flavoring, and preservatives

calcium mineral that your body needs to build strong bones and teeth. Calcium is found in dairy foods and some vegetables, nuts, and seeds.

calorie unit we use for measuring energy

carbohydrate substance in starchy foods (such as potatoes, pasta, and rice) and sugary foods that gives you energy

chemical substance made by mixing other substances together

coloring something added to food to make it look attractive

concentrate juice that has had most of the water taken out so that it lasts longer

digestive system all the body parts that break down food so the body can use it

fiber part of certain plants that passes through your body without being broken down. Fiber helps other foods to pass through your stomach, too. Some fiber can also help your blood stay healthy.

flavoring something added to food to make it taste better

lean describes meat that has little fat or has had the fatty parts trimmed off

mineral natural substance, such as iron, that is essential for health

nutrient substance in food that is good for your body, such as vitamins, minerals, and antioxidants

overweight heavier than is healthy for your age and height

poach cook using the method of simmering a whole piece of food (such as an egg or a fillet of fish) in water

preservative something added to food to make it last longer

processed made or prepared in a factory. Processed foods may contain artificial additives.

protein natural substance that your body needs to build skin, muscle, and other tissues. Protein is found in foods such as meat, fish, and beans.

saturated fat type of fat found in butter, fatty cuts of meat, cheese, and cream. It is bad for your heart and blood vessels.

sodium natural substance found in salt

vitamin natural substance that is essential for good health

whole grain made with every part of the grain, without removing any of the inner or outer parts

Find Out More

Books

Graimes, Nicola, and Howard Shooter. *Kids' Fun and Healthy Cookbook*. New York: Dorling Kindersley, 2007.

Parker, Vic. *All About Dairy (Food Zone)*. Irvine, Calif.: QEB, 2009.

Parker, Vic. *All About Grains (Food Zone)*. Irvine, Calif.: QEB, 2009.

Web sites

Facthound offers a safe, fun way to find Internet sites related to this book. All of the sites on Facthound have been researched by our staff.

Here's all you do:
Visit **www.facthound.com**
Type in this code: 9781432991166

Index